Contributed by
People in Law Enforcement Agencies
of the United States,
This Is

THE FIRST OFFICIAL
LAW ENFORCEMENT
COOKBOOK

Compiled by:
Nadine E. Anderberg

The First Official Law Enforcement Cookbook

Copyright © 1993 by Nadine E. Anderberg

Cover photography by Bret Anderberg

Published by R&E Publishers
P.O. Box 2008
Saratoga, California 95070

Printed in the United States of America

Additional copies of *The First Official Law Enforcement Cookbook* can be ordered for $7.95 plus $1.44 for postage and handling from:
Anderberg & Associates
40 Fourth St., Suite 103
Petaluma, California 94952

Make checks payable to **Anderberg & Associates**. Allow 4-6 weeks for delivery.

Contributions from the profits will be made to:

American Federation of Police Officers
3801 Biscayne Blvd.
N. Miami, Florida 33137

National Law Enforcement Officers Memorial
605 E Street N.W.
Washington, D.C. 20004

Dedication

Probably one of the most misunderstood professionals in our country is a law enforcement officer. Law enforcement has been the topic of hot television programs, best selling novels, and never-ending scrutiny and criticism.

Whether or not this profession deserves the often negative public recognition, two things remain: they are employed to serve and protect. For this I give my sincerest respect. They face a daily risk unnatural to the rest of us.

To those whose lives have been taken in the line of duty and to the loved ones who suffer and miss them still, I pay homage. To these people, I dedicate this cookbook.

Thank You!

Thanks to my family and friends, the dispatchers who spent *hours* locating addresses for me, and those who submitted recipes for this book.

I Confess!

This cookbook was born out of a need to spend less time in the kitchen but still get something out of it. To say I'm a cook is short of a criminal act. Just ask my brother, who, when I was 12 and he was 8 years old, ate my potato pancakes, which were quickly disposed of out the kitchen window into the subfreezing winter snow (they were still there the following spring). To this day if he hears the words "potato pancakes", he moans "ARGGGHH!", holds his stomach, squints his eyes, and puckers his lips. Born out of necessity, he became the cook in the family.

I also don't have the patience to cook gourmet-style and was sure there were other 'closet-fast-food-freaks' like me. When I was a police matron, I noticed that police officers ate on the run--or not at all! I figured we all could use a little help with 'kitchen quickies'. So, for the most part, the recipes in this book are under 45 minutes, including 5 minutes to eat--give or take 4 minutes!

Thus, I proclaim this--*The First Official Law Enforcement Cookbook*--to be fun, fast, and indigestion-free!

Happy cooking, healthy eating, and hey, let's be careful out there--in your kitchens!

Contents

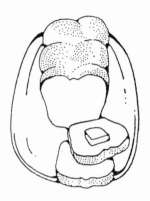

Breads

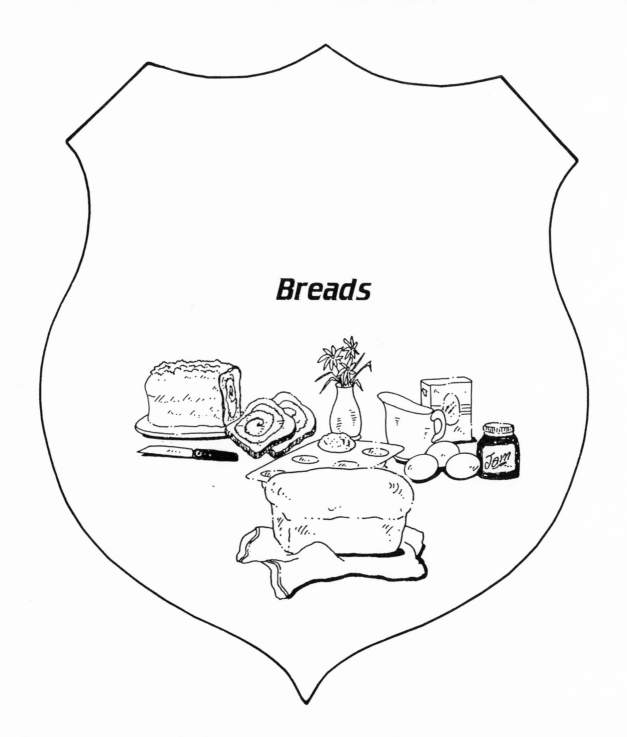

APPLESAUCE MUFFINS

Serves 6-8
Preparation time: 25 minutes

Philip Smith
Sergeant
Carnegie, Oklahoma

Ingredients:

2 cups flour
1 teaspoon baking soda
2 teaspoons cinnamon
1 teaspoon salt
2 eggs
1 cup oil
1 teaspoon vanilla
4 cups apples, peeled and chopped
1 cup nuts, chopped
2 cups raisins

Utensils:

Mixing bowl
Muffin pan
Oven, preheat to 350°

① In a bowl, mix the ingredients.

② Pour into ungreased muffin pan, 1/2 full. Bake for 15-20 minutes.

Substitutions: Flour with 1 cup wheat flour and 1 cup oatmeal; oil with 1/4 cup oil and 3/4 cup sugar; chopped apples with 1 pound 9 ounces applesauce.

BEER BREAD

Serves 4-6
Preparation time: 1-1/2 hours

Gene P. Plambeck
Sergeant
Cody, Wyoming

Ingredients:
3 cups flour
2-1/2 teaspoons baking powder
2 tablespoons sugar
Dash salt
1 can beer, room temperature

Utensils:
Mixing bowl
Loaf pan
Oven, preheat to 350°

①   In a bowl, mix the dry ingredients lightly with a spoon.

②   Pour in beer and beat 17-20 strokes. Do *not* overmix.

③   Pour batter in greased loaf pan and bake for 1-1/4 hours.

      Serve hot or cold, buttered or plain, with soup or sandwiches.

      For whole wheat variation: Substitute 1 cup whole wheat flour with 1 cup white flour, and add 4 ounces more of beer.

EASY MONKEY BREAD

Serves 6-8
Preparation time: 40 minutes

Sherry Glanz
Dispatcher
Yuma, Colorado

Ingredients:

1-1/2 cups sugar
1-3/4 teaspoons cinnamon
3, 10 ounce cans refrigerated buttermilk biscuits
1 stick (1/2 cup) margarine

Utensils:

Mixing bowl
Saucepan
9" bundt pan
Oven, preheat to 350°

①   Butter and flour bundt pan.

②   Mix together 1/2 cup of sugar and 1 teaspoon of cinnamon.

③   Cut biscuit dough in quarters. Roll each piece in cinnamon-sugar. Place loosely and evenly in bundt pan.

④   In saucepan, combine remaining sugar and cinnamon and margarine and stir until margarine melts. Pour evenly over dough in bundt pan.

⑤   Bake for 30 minutes. Cool in pan 5 minutes.

FLUFFY FRENCH TOAST

Serves 10-12
Preparation time: 20 minutes

Jodi Hanson
Dispatcher
Bismarck, North Dakota

Ingredients:

6 eggs
2 cups milk
1/2 cup flour
1-1/2 tablespoons sugar
1/4 teaspoon salt
18 slices French or white bread
1 tablespoon butter

Utensils:

Mixing bowl
Rotary beater
Frying pan

① In a bowl, beat eggs, milk, flour, sugar, and salt with beater until smooth.

② Soak bread in batter until saturated.

③ Melt butter in frying pan.

④ Fry each piece of bread over medium heat until golden brown.

FRENCH ROLLS

Serves 12-14
Preparation time: 3-1/2 hours

Ted Vastine
Chief of Police
Chadron, Nebraska

Ingredients:

2 packages dry yeast
2 cups warm water
1 teaspoon salt
2 teaspoons sugar
4 cups flour
Butter, melted
1 egg white, slightly beaten

Utensils:

Mixing bowl
Cookie sheet
Oven, preheat to 400°

①   In a bowl, mix the yeast, water, salt, and sugar.

②   Gradually add flour until dough is only slightly sticky. Knead for 5 minutes.

③   Cover and let rise until doubled, about 1-1/2 to 2 hours.

④   Shape into 18-24 oblong rolls and place on cookie sheet. Brush with butter and egg white. Cover and let rise until doubled, about 1 to 1-1/2 hours.

⑤   Bake for 25-30 minutes.

     Serve with chokecherry jelly.

13

ORANGE-CRANBERRY BREADS
Serves 4-6
Preparation time: 2 hours

Karen A. Bradford
Dispatcher
Smyrna, Tennessee

Ingredients:
2 tablespoons butter, creamed
2 cups sugar
1 egg
1/2 teaspoon baking soda
1/2 cup nuts, chopped
2 cups flour
3/4 cup orange juice
1 cup cranberries, cut in half
1 orange rind, grated

Utensils:
Mixing bowl
Loaf pan
Oven, preheat to 350°

①   In a bowl, mix ingredients.

②   Pour in loaf pan. Bake for 1-1/2 hours.

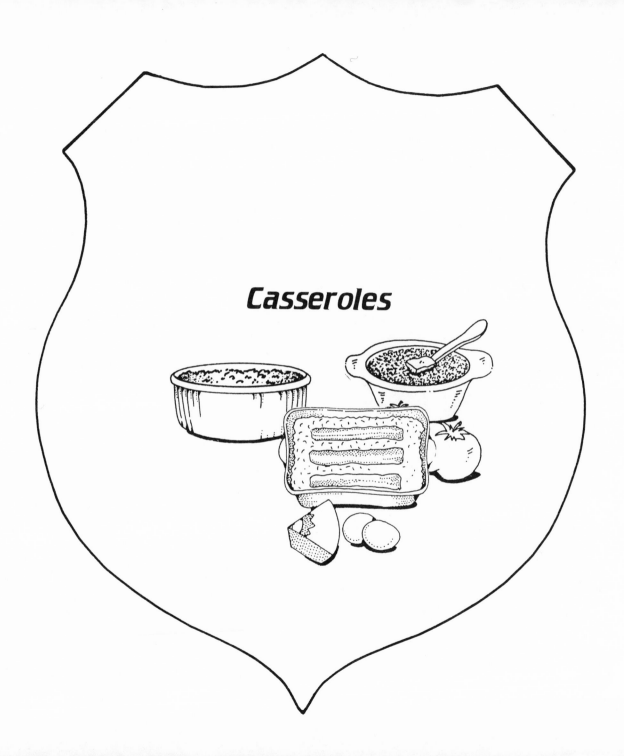

Casseroles

BREAKFAST CASSEROLE
Serves 4-6
Preparation time: 1-1/4 hours

Brian W. Hart
Detective
West Warwick, Rhode Island

Ingredients:
1 package cheddar cheese croutons
12 sausages (maple flavored is best), precooked
12 eggs
2-1/2 cups milk
1 package cheddar cheese, shredded
1/2 jar bacon bits

Utensils:
Large casserole dish
Blender
Oven, preheat to 325°

①   Line casserole dish with croutons. Top that with the sausages.

②   Blend the eggs and milk. Pour into casserole dish. Cover with cheddar cheese, then bacon bits.

③   Bake for 1 hour.

Variation: Use chunks of Polish ham instead of sausages.

CAMPFIRE STEW

Serves 4-6
Preparation time: 20 minutes

Doris Meredith Larson
Secretary to the Chief of Police
Pulaski, Virginia

Ingredients:

1 pound lean ground beef
1 can vegetable soup

Utensils:

Frying pan

①   Brown ground beef. Pour off drippings.

②   Add can of soup and heat.

          Serve with French bread and tossed salad.

CHARLIE'S CHILI

Serves 4-6
Preparation time: 1-1/2 hours

Charles M. Latham
Patrol Officer
Fulton, Missouri

Ingredients:

1-1/2 to 2 pounds ground beef
2 cans kidney beans
1 can tomato sauce
1 package chili seasoning
5 jalapeno peppers
1/2 onion, chopped
1/2 can beer (5% alcohol)
1 tablespoon tabasco sauce

Utensils:

Frying pan
Large soup kettle or
    crockpot

① Brown ground beef. Do not drain off drippings.

② In large pot, combine beef with remaining ingredients.

③ Cook on high for about 30 minutes, continuously stirring.

④ Reduce heat and simmer for 1 hour.

Variation: Put in crockpot on low for several hours.

Serve with scrambled eggs, toast, and milk.

19

CHILI

Tony Barthuly
Sergeant
Fond du Lac, Wisconsin

Serves 8-10
Preparation time: 2-1/2 hours

Ingredients:

3 pounds ground chuck
1 large onion, chopped
6 celery stalks, chopped
1, 46 ounce can V-8 juice
2, 16 ounce cans whole tomatoes
3, 8 ounce cans tomato sauce
3 tablespoons chili powder
1 tablespoon cumin
3 dashes tabasco sauce
1 teaspoon red peppers
2 bay leaves
1 teaspoon garlic powder
1 dash clove powder
2, 16 ounce cans kidney beans

Utensils:

Large frying pan
Large soup kettle

① Brown ground chuck.

② In large kettle, add browned chuck and remaining ingredients except kidney beans. Cook for 2 hours on medium to medium high.

③ Add kidney beans 1/2 hour before serving. Continue to heat on medium.

Serve topped with grated colby or cheddar cheese.

CHILI-CHEESE CASSEROLE

Serves 10-14
Preparation time: 1-1/4 hours

Lenora Viveros
Bureau Secretary
Ventura, California

Ingredients:

1 pound sharp cheddar cheese, grated
1 pound Jack cheese, grated
1, 27 ounce can whole green chilies, seeded
1, 7 ounce can chilies, chopped
2 cups milk
6 eggs
1 cup flour
Oregano, salt, and white pepper to taste

Utensils:

Mixing bowl
9" x 13" casserole dish
Oven, preheat to 350°

① In greased casserole dish, layer cheeses and whole chilies.

② In a bowl, mix the milk, eggs, flour, salt, and pepper. Pour over chili-cheese layers and top with chopped chilies.

③ Bake for 1 hour.

GARDEN SKILLET
Serves 2-4
Preparation time: 30 minutes

Peg Currier
Dispatcher
Newport, New Hampshire

Ingredients:

2 cups zucchini, diced
1/3 cup onion, chopped
1/2 teaspoon basil leaves, crushed
2 tablespoons butter
1, 11 ounce can condensed cheddar cheese soup
2 cups sharp cheddar cheese, shredded
1, 16 ounce can stewed tomatoes, drained and chopped
1/2 teaspoon prepared mustard
3 cups cooked elbow macaroni

Utensils:

Saucepan
Frying pan

① Prepare macaroni according to the package instructions.

② In the frying pan, cook zucchini, onion, basil, and butter until crispy and tender.

③ Add remaining ingredients, including the cooked macaroni. Heat and stir until cheese melts.

Serve with fresh, warm Italian or garlic bread.

22

HAMBURGER A LA CAMPBELL

Serves 4-6
Preparation time: 20 minutes

Bill Hatton
Lieutenant
Victoria, Texas

Ingredients:

3 pounds ground beef
1 can condensed mushroom soup
1/2 teaspoon onion powder
1/2 teaspoon garlic powder
1/2 teaspoon MSG
Instant rice, enough for 4-6 people
Salt and pepper to taste

Utensils:

Large frying pan
Large soup kettle

① Prepare rice according to the package instructions. Set aside.

② Brown ground beef. Add the onion and garlic powders, MSG, salt, pepper, and mushroom soup.

③ Stir until hot. Reduce heat and simmer.

Spoon over rice and serve with garlic toast and beer.

Variation: Add 1/2 to 1 cup sour cream to mixture and serve on noodles.

LOB-SCOUSE
Serves 4-6
Preparation time: 45 minutes

Doris Meredith Larson
Secretary to the Chief of Police
Pulaski, Virginia

Ingredients:

1 pound lean ground beef
4 potatoes, peeled and quartered
4 medium onions, peeled and sliced
Salt and pepper to taste

Utensils:

Large soup kettle
Potato masher

① In bottom of pot, place potatoes and onions. Spread ground beef on top and add enough water to cover all ingredients.

② Boil until vegetables are tender and meat is brown. Pour off and save excess water.

③ Mash meat and vegetables with potato masher, leaving some hunks of potato.

④ Pour in some of the excess water until you get a medium consistency (not so thin that it runs on a plate).

Serve with catsup, tossed salad, vegetables, and bread.

NOODLE DISH

Serves 4-6
Preparation time: 1 hour

Paul J. Feller
Captain
Dubuque, Iowa

Ingredients:

1 pound pork, cut in 1/2" cubes
1 pound beef, cut in 1/2" cubes
1 large onion, chopped
1 can cream style corn
1 can chicken noodle soup
2 tablespoons oil
2 tablespoons soy sauce
1 tablespoon sugar
1/2 teaspoon salt
1/4 teaspoon pepper
1 cup Ritz Crackers, crumbled
1 stick (1/2 cup) of margarine

Utensils:

3-quart dutch oven
Oven, preheat to 325°

① In dutch oven, heat oil until it's hot, then add onions and stir until onions become limp. Add meat and brown in the juice for 10-15 minutes. Pour off and reserve the juice. To the mixture, add the corn, soups (undiluted), sugar, salt, pepper, and soy sauce.

② To the reserved juice, add enough water to equal one cup. Add this to the above mixture a little at a time until it becomes the consistency of thick cream soup.

③ Prepare noodles according to the package instructions. Mix noodles with meat mixture and place in oven for 1/2 hour. Remove and cover with cracker crumbs, dot with margarine, and place back in oven for about 15 minutes or until the crackers are brown and crusty.

This will freeze well and is great reheated in the microwave.

25

PIZZA CASSEROLE
Serves 4-6
Preparation time: 1-1/4 hours

Inez Kashmark
Records Clerk Technician
Appleton, Minnesota

Ingredients:
1-1/2 pounds ground beef
1/2 cup onion, chopped
1/4 cup green olives, chopped
1 can mushrooms
1 teaspoon salt
1/2 teaspoon oregano
1/4 teaspoon pepper
1, 12 ounce package wide egg noodles
1 pint jar pizza sauce
2 cans tomato soup
1 cup milk
1 cup pepperoni, sliced
1, 8 ounce package mozarella cheese, shredded

Utensils:
Frying pan
4-quart baking dish
Saucepan
Oven, preheat to 350°

① Brown ground beef. Add onion, olives, mushrooms, and spices. Pour into baking dish.

② Prepare noodles according to the package instructions. Mix the noodles into the baking dish and the rest of the ingredients except the cheese.

③ Cover and bake for 45 minutes.

④ Sprinkle cheese over the top and bake, uncovered, for 15 minutes more.

Serve with tossed salad and warm French bread.

26

TACO HOT DISH
Serves 7-10
Preparation time: 1 hour

Coleen Isaak
Emergency Communications
Bismarck, North Dakota

Ingredients:
1, 12 ounce box Old El Paso Mexican Rice
1, 16 ounce can Old El Paso Refried Beans
1 pound ground beef
1 pound colby cheese, grated
1 head lettuce, shredded
4 medium size tomatoes, diced
4 raw green peppers, diced
2 medium size onions, diced
1 pound bag of Dorito corn chips, crumbled
Hot sauce to taste
1 pint sour cream

Utensils:
Medium saucepan
Frying pan
9" x 13" cake pan

① Prepare rice according to the package instructions.

② Brown ground beef. Mix in rice and beans and heat on the stove just until the mixture bubbles.

③ Spread heated mixture into the cake pan and top with cheese, lettuce, tomatoes, green peppers, onions, corn chips, hot sauce, and sour cream.

Desserts

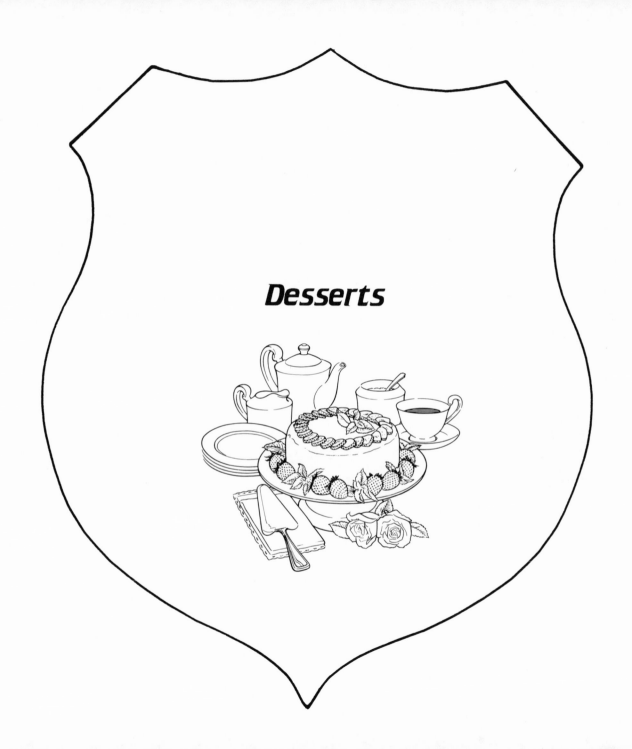

BREAD PUDDING DELIGHT

Serves 4
Preparation time: 15 minutes

Peg Currier
Dispatcher
Newport, New Hampshire

Ingredients:

1 package vanilla pudding mix
2 tablespoons sugar
3 cups milk
1/4 cup raisins
1 tablespoon butter
1/2 teaspoon vanilla extract
6 slices dry white bread, cut in 3/4" cubes
2 tablespoons sugar
1/4 teaspoon cinnamon
1/8 teaspoon nutmeg

Utensils:

Saucepan
Mixing bowl
Baking dish

① Combine pudding mix and sugar in saucepan. Blend in 2 cups of milk and raisins.

② Cook and stir over medium heat until mixture comes to a full boil. Remove from heat and stir in butter and vanilla.

③ Put bread crumbs in bowl and pour in remaining milk. Stir into pudding mixture and pour ingredients into baking dish.

④ Combine sugar, cinnamon, and nutmeg and sprinkle over pudding.

⑤ Broil until sugar is light brown and bubbly, about 4-5 minutes.

Serve warm or chilled.

31

CHOCOLATE MALT FROZEN DESSERT
Serves 10-15
Preparation time: 1-1/4 hours

Inez Kashmark
Records Clerk Technician
Appleton, Minnesota

Ingredients:
2 cups graham crackers, crushed
1/4 cup sugar
6 tablespoons margarine, melted
1/2 gallon vanilla ice cream, softened
2, 8 ounce packages malted milk balls, crushed
1 pint whipping cream, whipped
6 tablespoons marshmallow cream
6 tablespoons Nestles Quik

Utensils:
Mixing bowl
9" x 13" baking pan
Oven, preheat to 350°

① In a bowl, mix the graham crackers, sugar, and margarine.

② Press into pan and bake for 10 minutes. Cool.

③ In a bowl, fold 1 package malted milk balls into ice cream. Spread over cooled crust. Freeze for 1/2 hour.

④ Combine whipped cream, marshmallow cream, and Nestles Quik. Spread over ice cream layer. Top with 1/2 package of malted milk balls. Freeze for 1/2 hour.

CONGO BARS

Serves 10-12
Preparation time: 35 minutes

Karen A. Bradford
Dispatcher
Smyrna, Tennessee

Ingredients:

1 pound brown sugar
2/3 cup shortening, melted
3 eggs
2-2/3 cups flour
2-1/2 teaspoons baking powder
1/2 teaspoon salt
1 teaspoon vanilla
1 package chocolate chips
1 cup nuts, chopped

Utensils:

Mixing bowl
Cookie sheet
Oven, preheat to 350°

①   Mix ingredients. Batter will be stiff.

②   Spread on cookie sheet and bake for 25 minutes.

        Cool, then cut into squares.

FRUIT COCKTAIL CAKE
Serves 15-20
Preparation time: 50 minutes

John M. Cropper
Chief of Police
Ridgely, Maryland

Ingredients:
1-1/2 cups sugar
2 eggs
1/2 cup salad oil
2 cups flour
1/2 teaspoon salt
2 teaspoons baking soda
1, 8-3/4 ounce can fruit cocktail with juice
1/2 cup brown sugar

Utensils:
Mixing bowl
9" x 13" baking pan
Oven, preheat to 350°

① In a bowl, beat sugar, eggs, and oil. Add flour, salt, and baking soda, mixing well.

② Add fruit cocktail and stir. Pour batter into greased baking pan. Sprinkle brown sugar on top.

③ Bake for 45 minutes.

FRUIT DIP

Serves 8-10
Preparation time: 1 hour

Jodi Hanson
Dispatcher
Bismarck, North Dakota

Ingredients:

1 large jar marshmallow cream
2, 8 ounce packages cream cheese, softened
   (room temperature or microwave)

Utensils:

Mixing bowl
Electric mixer

①   In a bowl, beat ingredients until creamy.

②   Refrigerate for 45 minutes.

    Serve with bite-size pieces of mellon, strawberries, grapes, kiwi, cantaloup, etc.

FRUIT PIZZA

Serves 10-15
Preparation time: 35 minutes

Laura Mann
Operator
Bismarck, North Dakota

Ingredients:

1 roll Pillsbury Sugar Cookie dough
1 basket strawberries, sliced
1 jar strawberry glaze
2 kiwi fruits, sliced
1 can mandarine oranges
1 package cream cheese
1, 12 ounce container Cool Whip

Utensils:

Cookie sheet
Oven, preheat to 350°

①   Prepare cookies according to the package instructions. Cool.

②   Mix the cream cheese and Cool Whip. Spread on cooled cookies.

③   Place strawberry, orange, and kiwi slices on top.

④   Top with strawberry glaze.

Can be eaten immediately or chilled.

GOOEY BUTTER CAKE

Serves 15-20
Preparation time: 45 minutes

Ted Vastine
Chief of Police
Chadron, Nebraska

Ingredients:

1 package yellow cake mix (not pudding type)
1 stick (1/2 cup) butter
1 egg
1 tablespoon vanilla

Topping:
8 ounces cream cheese
1 pound box, minus 1/3 cup, powdered sugar
2 eggs

Utensils:

Blender
Mixing bowl
9" x 13" baking pan
Oven, preheat to 350°

① In blender, mix cake mix, butter, egg, and vanilla. Press into pan.

② In blender, mix cream cheese, powdered sugar, and eggs. Pour on top of cake.

③ Bake for 40 minutes.

Sprinkle with extra powdered sugar.

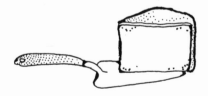

GRAPE-BLUEBERRY JELLO SALAD

Serves 4-6
Preparation time: 2-3 hours

William F. Gebauer
Assistant Chief
Medford, Wisconsin

Ingredients:

2, 3 ounce packages Concord Grape Jello
1, 20 ounce can crushed pineapple, including juice
1, 20 ounce can blueberry pie filling

Topping:
1 package cream cheese
1/2 cup sour cream
1/2 cup sugar
1 teaspoon vanilla
1 cup chopped nuts

Utensils:

Cake pan
Mixing bowl

① Mix Jello with 2 cups hot water. Pour in cake pan and cool.

② Add pineapple and blueberry pie filling to cooled Jello. Refrigerate until hard.

③ Mix ingredients for topping and spread over Jello mixture. Top with chopped nuts.

Keep refrigerated.

MINNEHAHA CAKE

Barbara Jordan
Dispatcher
Campbell, Missouri

Serves 15-20
Preparation time: 1 hour

Ingredients:

2 cups margarine or butter
2 cups packed brown sugar
4 eggs, separated
2 cups cornmeal
2 cups unbleached or all-purpose flour
1 tablespoon baking powder
1 cup milk
1 tablespoon ginger root, freshly grated
1/2 cup raisins
1 cup currants
1/4 cup citron or dried fruit, finely chopped
Dash of nutmeg, freshly grated

Utensils:

Electric beater
Mixing bowl
9" x 13" x 2" baking pan
Oven, preheat to 350°

① Beat egg whites until stiff. Set aside.

② Beat margarine with sugar until fluffy. Beat egg yolks and add to margarine mixture.

③ Combine flour, cornmeal, and baking powder. Add cornmeal mixture to egg mixture, alternating with milk. Stir in raisins, currants, ginger, and citron.

④ Fold in egg whites. Pour into greased baking pan.

⑤ Bake for 35 minutes. Cover with foil and bake 15 minutes more.

SWISS CHOCOLATE SQUARES

Serves 15-20
Preparation time: 25 minutes

Rocky Jacobs
Records Clerk
Flagstaff, Arizona

Ingredients:

1 cup water
1/2 cup margarine
5 tablespoons cocoa powder
2 cups flour
2 cups sugar
2 eggs
1/2 cup sour cream
1 teaspoon soda
1/2 teaspoon salt

Icing:
1/2 cup margarine, melted
6 (or more) tablespoons milk
1 teaspoon vanilla

Utensils:

Saucepan
Mixing bowl
15-1/2" x 10-1/2" jelly roll
    pan or cookie sheet
Oven, preheat to 375°

5 tablespoons cocoa powder
4-1/2 cups powdered sugar
1 cup nuts, chopped
Dash salt

①   Combine water, margarine, and cocoa in saucepan and bring to a boil. Remove from heat and cool.

②   In a bowl, combine the ingredients from step 1 and the flour, sugar, eggs, sour cream, soda and salt. Mix well.

③   Pour onto greased cookie sheet. Bake for 20-25 minutes.

④   In a bowl, combine the icing ingredients and mix well. Spread on warm cake.

⑤   Cool in refrigerator, then cut into 1" pieces.

WHOOPIE PIES

Serves 10-12
Preparation time: 20 minutes

Karen A. Bradford
Dispatcher
Smyrna, Tennessee

Ingredients:

1 cup sugar
1/2 cup shortening
2 egg yolks (save egg whites)
1 cup milk
2 cups flour
1 teaspoon baking powder
1 teaspoon salt
1 teaspoon baking soda
6 tablespoons Hershey's Cocoa
2 cups powdered sugar

Filling:
2 egg whites
1/2 teaspoon vanilla
1/2 cup shortening

Utensils:

Mixing bowl
Cookie sheet
Electric mixer
Oven, preheat to 350°
Wax paper

① Sift flour, baking powder, salt, baking soda, and cocoa. Mix together with sugar, egg yolks, shortening, and milk.

② Drop by tablespoonfuls onto greased cookie sheet. Bake for 10 minutes and cool.

③ Beat filling ingredients. Frost between 2 cakes.

Wrap individually in wax paper.

41

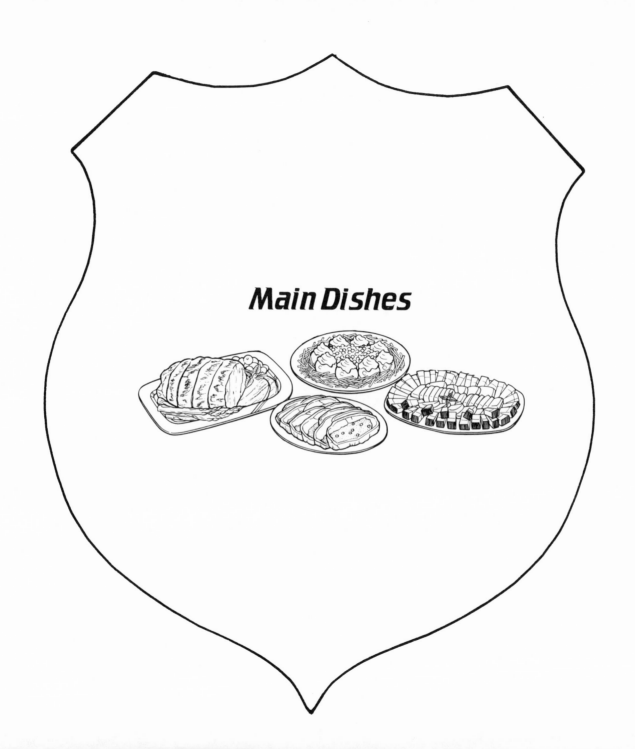

Main Dishes

BAKED CHICKEN & RICE

Serves 4-6
Preparation time: 1-1/2 hours

Lila Ashenbrenner
Lieutenant
Hillsboro, Oregon

Ingredients:

6 chicken breasts, halved
1/4 cup flour
Dash paprika
1 teaspoon salt
1/4 cup margarine
1/4 teaspoon pepper
3-4 cubes chicken bouillon
2 tablespoons onion, chopped
2 cups regular rice, uncooked

Utensils:

Shaking bag
Baking dish
Oven, preheat to 400°

① Put flour, paprika, salt and pepper in bag and shake chicken pieces.

② Melt margarine in shallow baking dish.

③ Place chicken in baking dish, skin side down. Bake 20 minutes.

④ Remove from oven and remove chicken from dish.

⑤ Put onion, rice, and 4 cups boiling water in dish. Place chicken back in, skin side up.

⑥ Bake for 40 minutes more.

Sprinkle with paprika.

BEEF STEW

Serves 4-6
Preparation time: 1 hour

Joan P. Carey
Secretary
Mineral Point, Wisconsin

Ingredients:

2 pounds beef chuck, cut into cubes
2 tablespoons salad oil
1 medium onion, chopped
1 package beef stew seasoning mix
1-2 packages beef gravy mix
6 carrots, sliced
6 potatoes, sliced

Utensils:

Frying pan

① Brown meat in oil. Add stew seasoning mix according to package instructions. Simmer while preparing vegetables.

② Add gravy mix and stir until dissolved. For thicker stew, add another package.

③ Add vegetables and cook until tender.

Variation: Use canned vegetables instead of fresh; this will reduce cooking time.

CHICKEN BREASTS PIQUANT

Serves 4-6
Preparation time: 40 minutes

Mary Ellen O'Connor
Senior Clerk
Beverly, Massachusetts

Ingredients:

4-6 chicken breasts
1 cup rose or dry red wine
1/2 cup soy sauce
1/2 cup salad oil
4 tablespoons water
1/2 teaspoon oregano
2 tablespoons brown sugar
1/2 teaspoon garlic powder

Utensils:

13" x 9" baking pan
Mixing bowl
Oven, preheat to 375°

① Arrange chicken in pan.

② In a bowl, combine remaining ingredients. Pour over chicken.

③ Cover and bake for 30 minutes.

Serve with rice.

You can refrigerate or freeze the uncooked dish until you want to bake it.

47

CHIEF'S CAJUN CORN SOUP
Serves 8-10
Preparation time: 1-1/2 hours

Norman R. "Nookie" Diaz
Chief of Police
Thibodaux, Louisiana

Ingredients:
3 large onions, chopped
1/2 bell pepper, chopped
2 ribs celery, chopped
1 tablespoon oil
1, 12 ounce can rotel tomatoes
5 cups water
1 quart fresh corn, cut from 12 cobs
1-1/2 pounds shrimp, peeled and deveined
1 pound ham, cut in cubes
2, 8 ounce cans tomato sauce

Utensils:
Large soup kettle

4 ounces thin spaghetti,
  cooked
1 teaspoon parsley
1 tablespoon seasoned salt
1 tablespoon creole seasoning
1 teaspoon chili powder
2 cloves garlic, chopped
Salt and pepper to taste

① In soup kettle, brown onions, bell pepper, and celery in oil. Add tomatoes and saute until tender.

② Add small amounts of water, stirring constantly over medium heat. Cook 15 minutes.

③ Add corn, shrimp, and ham and cook until shrimp turns pink, about 15 minutes more.

④ Add tomato sauce and remaining water. Bring to a boil. Reduce heat and simmer 30 minutes.

⑤ Add spaghetti, parsley, garlic, and seasoning.

Serve with cornbread.

CHIEF'S DISH

Serves 4
Preparation time: 1-1/2 hours

Norman R. "Nookie" Diaz
Chief of Police
Thibodaux, Louisiana

Ingredients:

1 chicken, broiled and deboned
12 ounces vermicelli, cooked
2, 3 ounce cans mushrooms
1/4 cup pimento
1 cup green peppers, chopped
2 cups Pet milk
1 can cream of mushroom soup
1/2 cup margarine
1 cup onions, chopped
1 cup celery, chopped
1 cup green onions, chopped
16 ounces Velvetta cheese
1 teaspoon garlic powder
1 teaspoon salt
Tabasco to taste

Utensils:

Large casserole dish
Saucepan
Oven, preheat to 350°

① Melt 1/2 of the cheese, soup, and milk. Add garlic, salt, pimento, and tabasco. Add chicken and vermicelli.

② Pour ingredients into greased casserole dish.

③ Grate rest of cheese and put over top.

④ Cover and bake for 1 hour.

49

CHIEF'S HOT ANTIPASTA WITH LINGUINI

Serves 4
Preparation time: 20 minutes

Edward Hayes
Chief of Police
Peekskill, New York

Ingredients:

2-4 cloves garlic, chopped
1/4 cup olive oil
1/2 cup black olives, pitted
1/2 cup stuffed green olives
6 ounce jar artichoke hearts
7 ounce jar roasted red peppers, chopped
1/2 cup dry white wine
14-1/2 ounce can chicken broth
1 cup mushrooms, sliced
1/2 teaspoon oregano
1/4 teaspoon basil
1/8 teaspoon black pepper
1/4 teaspoon crushed red pepper
1 pound linguini noodles

Utensils:

6 quart saucepan
3 quart saucepan
Frying pan

One or more of the following:
1-1/2 pounds raw shelled
  shrimp
1-1/2 pounds scallops
1-1/2 pounds imitation
  seafood
3 cans clams, chopped
3 cans tuna in water
1-1/2 pounds chicken, cubed
1-1/2 pounds veal, cubed

① Saute garlic, adding seafood or meat. Remove from heat.

② Boil 6 quarts of water and cook linguini.

③ In a 3 quart saucepan, heat remaining ingredients. Add contents of skillet and simmer about 10 minutes.

Serve with grated Parmesan cheese, garlic bread, salad, and beer or wine.

CHUNG DUNG LUNG

Serves 2
Preparation time: 20 minutes

Scott A. Stookey
Patrol Officer
Stillwater, Oklahoma

Ingredients:

1 green pepper, cut into thin strips
1 large yellow onion, cut into thin strips
1 pound round steak, cut into thin strips
2 tablespoons corn starch
1 carrot, cut into thin strips
1 cup beef bouillon
1 clove garlic, smashed with the side of a knife
1 cup bean sprouts
2 tablespoons lemon juice
3 tablespoons soy sauce
3/4 cups cooking oil

Utensils:

Wok or deep frying pan
Mixing bowl

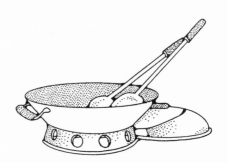

① Make bouillon and cool. Add corn starch and 1 tablespoon soy sauce and set aside.

② Combine lemon juice, 2 tablespoons soy sauce, 1/4 cup oil, and beef broth for a marinate.

③ Heat 1/4 cup oil in wok. Slowly add beef. Cook about 3 minutes, or until it turns gray. Remove the beef and put in the marinate.

④ Stir-fry onions, peppers, and carrots for about 2 minutes. Add garlic and 1/4 cup water. Stir for 4 minutes until tender and crisp. Add the beef and remaining ingredients and stir until liquid thickens.

Serve on rice.

51

CROCKPOT RIBS
Serves 4-6
Preparation time: 5-6 hours

Ted Vastine
Chief of Police
Chadron, Nebraska

Ingredients:

3-5 pounds ribs
1/2 cup catsup
1/4 cup water
2 tablespoons brown sugar
2 tablespoons Worcestershire sauce
2 tablespoons grated onion
2 tablespoons vinegar
1/2 teaspoon salt
1/4 teaspoon chili powder
1/8 teaspoon garlic powder
1/8 teaspoon pepper
Tabasco sauce to taste

Utensils:

Crockpot

①   Put ribs in bottom of crockpot and cover with ingredients.

②   Cook on high for 5-6 hours.

CURRIED SHRIMP

Serves 4-6
Preparation time: 30 minutes

Stephanie D. Yutzie
Records Clerk
Walla Walla, Washington

Ingredients:

3-4 cups cooked rice or noodles
1 pound cleaned raw shrimp
1 cup onion, chopped
1/4 cup butter
5 tablespoons flour
1 teaspoon salt
1-1/2 teaspoons curry powder
1/2 teaspoon sugar
1/8 teaspoon ginger
1-1/2 teaspoons chicken bouillon (dry)
1-1/2 cups hot water
1/2 teaspoon lemon juice
2 tablespoons sherry

Utensils:

Microwave
Microwave dish

① In microwave, cook celery, onion, and butter on high for 4 minutes. Stir and microwave 4 more minutes. Add flour, salt, curry powder, sugar, ginger, and microwave on high for 1 minute.

② Combine chicken bouillon and hot water and add to mixture. Cook in microwave on high for 5 minutes.

③ Add shrimp and lemon juice. Cook in microwave on low for 7 minutes. Stir and cook for 7 minutes more.

④ Remove and add sherry.

Serve over rice or noodles.

53

EASY RAVIOLI

Serves 4-6
Preparation time: 45 minutes

Thelma Poll
Identification Clerk
Wyoming, Michigan

Ingredients:

1, 12 ounce can ravioli
1 pound ground beef
1 tablespoon onion, chopped
1 cup cheddar or mozzerella cheese, or 1/2 of each, shredded
1 small can sliced mushrooms
Garlic salt to taste

Utensils:

Microwave
8" x 8" glass baking dish
Frying pan

①   In the bottom of the glass baking dish, carefully arrange ravioli squares.

②   Brown ground beef, seasoning with garlic salt. Add onion and cook until done; drain well. An alternative is to scatter onion over top of cheese along with a few sliced mushrooms instead of frying onion with the meat.

③   Spread ground beef over top of ravioli and top with the shredded cheese.

④   Microwave for 5-8 minutes on high or until cheese melts.

FANCY FAST CHICKEN

Serves 2-3
Preparation time: 1-1/4 hours

Mary Ellen O'Connor
Senior Clerk
Beverly, Massachusetts

Ingredients:

3 chicken breasts
6 slices swiss cheese
1/4 cup mushrooms, slices
1, 10-3/4 ounce can cream of chicken soup
1/2 cup white wine
2 cups Pepperidge Farm stuffing
1 stick (1/2 cup) butter, melted

Utensils:

Mixing bowl
9" x 13" glass dish
Oven, preheat to 350°

①   Place chicken in glass dish.

②   Top each piece with cheese. Top cheese with mushrooms.

③   In a bowl, mix soup and wine. Pour over chicken.

④   Spread stuffing over top and drizzle with melted butter.

⑤   Bake for 50-55 minutes.

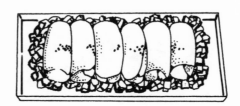

FRICASSE PORK CHOPS
Serves 4-6
Preparation time: 45 minutes

Thelma Poll
Identification Clerk
Wyoming, Michigan

Ingredients:

4-6 lean pork chops
1, 12 ounce can Campbell's Chicken with Rice soup
1, 16 ounce box Minute Rice

Utensils:

Microwave
Microwave dish
Frying pan
Medium saucepan

①   Place one pork chop at a time on the microwave dish, cover with plastic wrap and cook on high for 1 minute or until partially cooked.

②   Brown all of the pork chops, then cover pork chops with can of soup (do not add water). Simmer for approximately 20-30 minutes or until done.

       If any liquid remains, add one or two tablespoons of Minute Rice to absorb the liquid.

③   Prepare Minute Rice according to the package instructions.

       Serve with greenbeans and coleslaw with either chopped pineapple or apple.

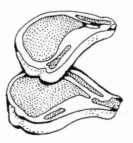

GAS BLAST
Serves 4-6
Preparation time: 15 minutes

Bret Anderberg
Patrol Officer
Bloomington, Minnesota

Ingredients:

1 pound ground beef
1 onion, chopped fine
1, 12 ounce can pork 'n beans
3 ounces Ortega Hot Taco Sauce

Utensils:

Frying pan

①   Brown meat and drain.

②   Mix in remaining ingredients and simmer 10 minutes.

57

GRILLED FISH

Serves 2
Preparation time: 35 minutes

Ayad N. Zako
Patrol Officer
San Jose, California

Ingredients:

2 pieces red snapper filet
4 medium red-skin potatoes, quartered
4 carrots, cut in 1/2" pieces
1 lemon, squeezed
1 cup white table wine
Salt and pepper to taste
Dash cayenne pepper
1-2 tablespoons salad oil

Utensils:

Grill, gas or coal
Microwave
Microwave dish
Saucepan

① Start up the grill.

② Marinate fish in lemon juice, wine, oil, and cayenne pepper. Set aside.

③ Boil potatoes in pot of water for 15-20 minutes.

④ Place carrots in dish half covered with water and microwave on high for 15 minutes.

⑤ Make sure the grill is hot. Grill fish for 2-1/2 to 3 minutes on each side.

Serve with potatoes and carrots.

GROUND BEEF AND RICE SOUP

Serves 10
Preparation time: 50 minutes

Rosalie Buehrer
Cook, County Sheriff's Department
Leland, Michigan

Ingredients:

1 pound ground beef
3 beef bouillon cubes
6 cups hot water
2, 1 pound cans stewed or regular tomatoes
2, 1-3/8 ounce envelopes dry onion soup mix
1 cup celery, diced
1 teaspoon oregano leaf
1/2 cup uncooked white rice

Utensils:

Large soup pot

① In a pot, crumble beef and cook over moderate heat, stirring until beef is browned.

② Add remaining ingredients and bring mixture to a boil.

③ Reduce heat and simmer 40-45 minutes.

Serve with crackers and salad or coleslaw and baked custard for dessert.

HAMBURGER PIE

Serves 4-6
Preparation time: 45 minutes

Carl Stennes
Detention Officer
Wolf Point, Montana

Ingredients:

1/2 cup tomato sauce
1/2 cup bread crumbs
1 pound ground beef
1/4 cup onion, chopped
1/4 cup green pepper, chopped
1-1/2 teaspoons salt
1/8 teaspoon oregano
1/8 teaspoon pepper

Filling:
1-1/3 cups Minute Rice, dry
1 cup water
1-1/2 cups tomato sauce
1 cup cheddar cheese, grated
1/2 teaspoon salt

Utensils:

Mixing bowl
Pie plate
Oven, preheat to 350°

① In a bowl, combine ingredients, mixing well. Press into pie plate and set aside.

② In a bowl, combine filling ingredients and only 1/4 cup cheddar cheese. Spoon into meat shell, and cover with foil.

③ Bake for 25 minutes.

④ Sprinkle with remaining cheese and bake uncovered 10-15 minutes more.

JIM'S MEATLOAF
Serves 4-6
Preparation time: 4-5 hours

James B. Simmerman
Chief of Police
Marshall, Missouri

Ingredients:

1 pound ground beef or steak
1 egg
2-4 shakes soy sauce
Dash of liquid smoke
1 cup bread crumbs
1/2 cup onion, chopped

Utensils:

Crockpot

①   Combine ingredients and form into ball or loaf.

②   Cook on low in crockpot for 4-5 hours.

     Variation: Put in loaf pan and cook in oven at 375° for 1 hour.

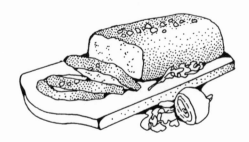

JIM'S ONE POT DINNER
Serves 4-6
Preparation time: 4-8 hours

James B. Simmerman
Chief of Police
Marshall, Missouri

Ingredients:
1 pound ground beef
1 can lima beans
2 cans kidney beans
1 can pork 'n beans
1 teaspoon liquid smoke
1 teaspoon soy sauce
3 tablespoons white vinegar
1 cup catsup or barbeque sauce
1/2 cup onion, chopped
4 ounces Bacos

Utensils:
Frying pan
Crockpot

①   Brown ground beef.

②   Combine beef with remaining ingredients in crockpot. Cook on low for 4-8 hours.

MEXICAN MEATLOAF
Serves 4-6
Preparation time: 1-1/4 hours

Don Jackson
Sergeant
Buckeye, Arizona

Ingredients:

1 cup onion, chopped
1/2 cup green pepper, chopped
1 clove garlic, chopped
1 tablespoon chili powder
1 cup water
1 pound ground beef
1/2 cup cornmeal
1-1/2 teaspoons salt
1/8 teaspoon pepper
3/4 cup catsup
3 eggs
2 teaspoons Worcestershire sauce
2 tablespoons butter

Utensils:

Frying pan
Loaf pan
Oven, preheat to 350°

① Saute onion, green pepper, garlic, and chili powder in butter until vegetables are tender. Mix in remaining ingredients and only 1/2 cup catsup.

② Shape into a loaf and place in loaf pan. Cover with remaining catsup.

③ Bake for 1 hour.

63

QUICKY RELLENOS

Serves 2-4
Preparation time: 50 minutes

Don Jackson
Sergeant
Buckeye, Arizona

Ingredients:
2 cups longhorn cheese, grated
2 cups milk
3 eggs
1/2 cup flour
2, 4 ounce cans whole green chilies

Utensils:
Mixing bowl
Casserole dish
Oven, preheat to 350°

①   In a bowl, mix eggs, milk, and flour.

②   In a greased casserole dish, layer chilies and then cheese. Top it off with the milk mixture.

③   Bake uncovered for 45 minutes.

SPAGHETTI SAUCE
Serves 6-8
Preparation time: 25 minutes

Don Jackson
Sergeant
Buckeye, Arizona

Ingredients:
1 box spaghetti noodles
1 cup celery, diced
2 cloves garlic, minced and pressed
4 tablespoons oil
2, 16 ounce cans stewed or chopped tomatoes
1 cup tomato soup
1-1/2 teaspoons salt
1 teaspoon dried basil leaves, crumbled
1/2 teaspoon thyme
1/2 teaspoon oregano leaves, crumbled
1/4 cup green peppers, chopped
1/2 cup burgundy
4 teaspoons parsley

Utensils:
Saucepan
Frying pan

① Prepare noodles according to package instructions, enough for 6-8 people.

② Saute celery, onion, green pepper, and garlic in oil until tender but not brown.

③ Add tomatoes, tomatoe soup, salt, pepper, and herbs. Bring to a boil. Simmer uncovered for 15 minutes.

④ Add burgundy and parsley and return to boil.

Serve over noodles.

Variation: Add Italian sausage, ground beef, or any other meat.

65

TURKEY IN A SKILLET
Serves 4-6
Preparation time: 40 minutes

Jack L. Dillon
Chief Deputy
Washington, Iowa

Ingredients:
1 pound ground turkey
1 large onion, chopped
1 cup carrots, diced
1 cup small shell macaroni
1 can french green beans
1 small can mushrooms
1 can stewed tomatoes
1/2 teaspoon cumin powder
Ground red peppers, salt, and pepper to taste

Utensils:
Frying pan

① Brown the turkey and onion. Drain off excess grease.

② Add remaining ingredients except red peppers. Cover and bring to boil. Reduce heat and simmer for 30 minutes.

   Variation: Add potatoes, whole kernel corn, etc.

③ Add the red pepper.

   Variation: Add Louisiana hot sauce or cayenne pepper.

WAFFLES
Serves 2
Preparation time: 20 minutes

Scott A. Stookey
Patrol Officer
Stillwater, Oklahoma

Ingredients:

2-1/4 cups all-purpose flour
4 teaspoons baking powder
1/2 teaspoon salt
3 tablespoons sugar
2 eggs
2 cups milk
1/2 cup oil
2 tablespoons vanilla
1/4 cup oatmeal
1 can blueberries, drained

Utensils:

Mixing bowl
Waffle iron, preheat
Electric mixer

①   Blend the ingredients.

②   Pour batter into waffle iron until it's 1/2 full. Cook about 2 minutes.

     Serve with butter and syrup.

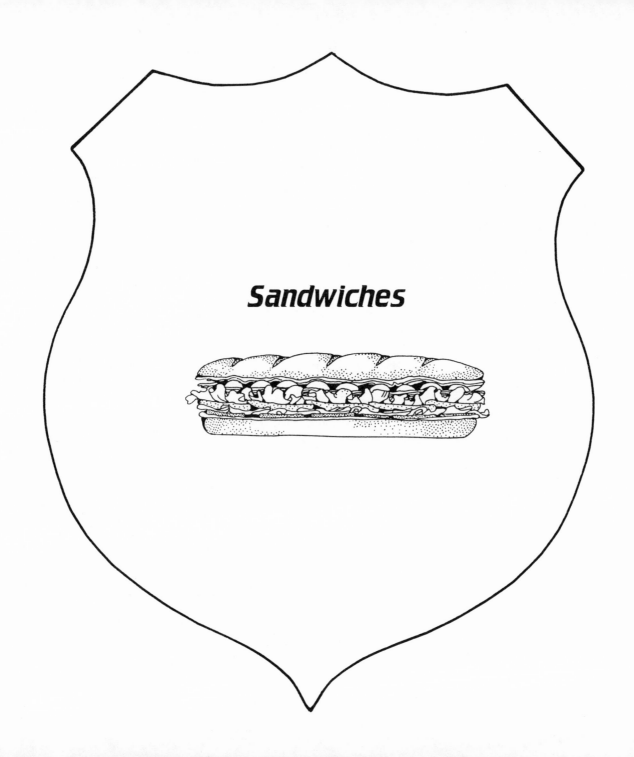

Sandwiches

ARCTIC SHRIMP SALAD SANDWICH FILLING

Serves 4-6
Preparation time: 5 minutes

Lawrence A. Wallace
Captain
Kotzebue, Alaska

Ingredients:

2, 4 ounce cans small shrimp, finely diced
1, 8 ounce package cream cheese, room temperature
8 ounces mayonnaise
4 ounces concentrated lemon juice
1 ounce lemon rind, minced
1/2 cup celery, finely chopped
1/2 cup green onion, finely chopped

Utensils:

Large mixing bowl
Electric mixer

① In a large mixing bowl, combine ingredients.

② Mix with an electric mixer at high speed.

Serve between pieces of bread or as a dip with chips, crackers, or vegetables.

Can be served immediately but tastes better chilled for several hours.

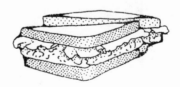

BARBEQUE
Serves 6-8
Preparation time: 35 minutes

Joan P. Carey
Secretary
Mineral Point, Wisconsin

Ingredients:

2 pounds ground beef
2/3 cup onion, chopped
1 teaspoon salt
1/8 teaspoon pepper
1, 10-1/2 ounce can tomato soup
1, 10-1/2 ounce can chicken gumbo soup

Utensils:

Frying pan

①   Brown ground beef. Add onion and cook until browned.

②   Stir in remaining ingredients. Simmer for 30 minutes.

Serve on hamburger buns with catsup and mustard.

Variation: Simmer in crockpot until ready to eat.

BOWLING ALLEY B.B.Q.'S

Serves 6-8
Preparation time: 20 minutes

Jodi Hanson
Dispatcher
Bismarck, North Dakota

Ingredients:

3 pounds ground beef
1/2 cup chili sauce
1 small bottle catsup
2 teaspoons horseradish
1 can chicken gumbo soup
1 tablespoon brown sugar
1 onion, chopped

Utensils:

Frying pan

①   Brown ground beef. Drain fat.

②   Add remaining ingredients and simmer on low for 15 minutes.

      Serve on hamburger buns or eat plain.

HOT BEEF SANDWICH

Serves 6-8
Preparation time: 3-1/2 to 4 hours

Joan P. Carey
Secretary
Mineral Point, Wisconsin

Ingredients:

3-4 pounds chuck roast, cut into cubes
1 package dry onion soup mix
1 cube beef bouillon
1 cup hot water
Flour to thicken

Utensils:

Mixing bowl
Baking dish
Oven, preheat to 300°

① Dissolve bouillon in hot water. Add soup mix.

② Put roast cubes in baking dish. Pour ingredients on top.

③ Cover and bake for 3-1/2 to 4 hours.

④ Add flour to thicken.

Serve on hamburger buns, bread, or eat plain.

Variation: Mash ingredients with potato masher instead of using flour to thicken. Also add 2 tablespoons Worcestershire sauce or barbeque sauce.

HOT SPAMWICH

Serves 4-6
Preparation time: 25 minutes

Joan P. Carey
Secretary
Mineral Point, Wisconsin

Ingredients:

4-6 hamburger buns
1 can Spam, ground
1 cup mild American cheese, diced
1 small onion, diced
4 tablespoons pickles or pickle relish
4 tablespoons butter, melted
4 tablespoons milk
2 tablespoons catsup
2 tablespoons green pepper, chopped

Utensils:

Mixing bowl
Aluminum foil
Cookie sheet
Oven, preheat to 375°

① In a bowl, mix ingredients. Spread on buns and wrap in foil.

② Bake 20 minutes.

Keeps in refrigerator for several days. Remove foil and reheat in microwave.

MINI PIZZAS

Serves 1
Preparation time: 15 minutes

Jodi Hanson
Dispatcher
Bismarck, North Dakota

Ingredients:

1 slice bread or English muffin
1-2 tablespoons pizza sauce
Toppings of your choice
1-2 tablespoons mozzarella cheese, grated

Utensils:

Cookie sheet
Oven, preheat to 450°

①   Spread pizza sauce on slice of bread or muffin. Add topping.

②   Bake for 5 minutes.

③   Sprinkle cheese on top. Bake 5 minutes more or until cheese melts.

For crispy pizza crust, butter bread or muffin lightly on the bottom or toast before spreading pizza sauce on top.

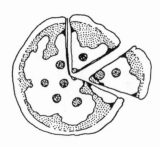

PICKLE BURGERS

Serves 4
Preparation time: 15 minutes

Jodi Hanson
Dispatcher
Bismarck, North Dakota

Ingredients:

1 pound ground beef
1 dill pickle, chopped
1 tablespoon onion, grated
1/2 teaspoon salt
Lawry's salt to taste

Utensils:

Mixing bowl
Broiler pan

①   In a bowl, combine all ingredients.

②   Shape into patties. Sprinkle with Lawry's salt.

③   Broil for 5 minutes on each side or until done.

       Serve on hamburger buns or eat plain.

77

PITA POCKET SURPRISE

Serves 2
Preparation time: 1 hour

Lisa Michaelis
Patrol Officer
Monroe, Connecticut

Ingredients:

1 pound chicken or turkey, boneless and skinless,
    cut into 1/2" pieces
2 cups (any) vegetable, chopped
1, 7 ounce box Near East rice or Rice-a-Roni
1 pita pocket bread

Utensils:

Saucepans

①   Prepare rice according to the package instructions.

②   In a saucepan, put meat on bottom and just enough water to cover. Simmer on low heat for 45 minutes.

③   Add vegetables to cooked rice and simmer for 5 minutes.

④   Drain water from meat and add rice mixture.

Serve stuffed in a pita pocket bread or as a dinner dish with applesauce or salad.

Variation: Use pasta instead of rice or tofu instead of chicken/turkey.

RIB STICKER

Serves 1
Preparation time: 5 minutes

Linda Lovchuk
Sergeant
Grand Rapids, Michigan

Ingredients:

2 Slices Brownberry whole wheat bread
1 egg
1 teaspoon margarine
3-4 tablespoons of peanut butter

Utensils:

Frying pan

① In frying pan, melt margarine and fry the egg, breaking the yolk.

② Spread peanut butter on lightly toasted bread. Slap the fried egg on top of the peanut butter side of the sandwich and place the other slice on top.

Serve with ice cold milk or hot coffee.

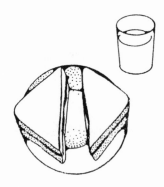

SLOPPY JOES

Serves 4-6
Preparation time: 1 hour

Paul J. Feller
Captain
Dubuque, Iowa

Ingredients:

2 pounds ground beef
1 medium onion, chopped
1, 14 ounce bottle of catsup
2 tablespoons brown sugar
1 tablespoon chili powder
2 tablespoons flour, mixed in 3/4 cup cold water
1 can corned beef, broken with fork
6-8 hamburger buns

Utensils:

Large frying pan

① In frying pan, brown ground beef and onions. Drain.

② Stir in catsup, brown sugar, chili powder, and flour mixture.

③ Mix in broken up corned beef.

④ Cover and simmer for 45 minutes, stirring occasionally.

Serve on hamburger buns.

This can be frozen and reheated in the microwave.

TORTILLA PIZZA

Serves 8-10
Preparation time: 20 minutes

Denise A. Jenter
Secretary, Records Section
Sturgis, South Dakota

Ingredients:

1 package flour tortillas (6-7" diameter)
1 small jar Ragu Pizza sauce
1, 8 ounce package mozzarella cheese, shredded

Toppings:
Pepperoni, olives, onions, mushrooms, green peppers, shrimp, etc.

Utensils:

Cookie sheet
Aluminum foil
Oven, preheat to 425°

① Cover the cookie sheet with foil. Put tortillas on top.

② Spoon 2 tablespoons of pizza sauce on top of each tortilla. Add cheese and your favorite topping.

③ Bake for 10 minutes.

Serve with salad.

VEGIE PIZZA

Serves 3-5
Preparation time: 20 minutes

Laura Mann
Operator
Bismarck, North Dakota

Ingredients:

1 roll refrigerator pizza dough
1 package Hidden Valley Ranch powder salad dressing
3 tablespoons mayonnaise
1, 8 ounce package cream cheese
1 head of broccoli, break off tops and chop
1 package cheese, shredded
1 green pepper, chopped

Utensils:

Cookie sheet
Oven, preheat to 350°

①　　Prepare pizza dough according to the package instructions. Cool.

②　　Mix powder salad dressing, mayonnaise, and cream cheese.

③　　Spread over pizza crust. Top with broccoli, green pepper, and cheese.

Side Dishes

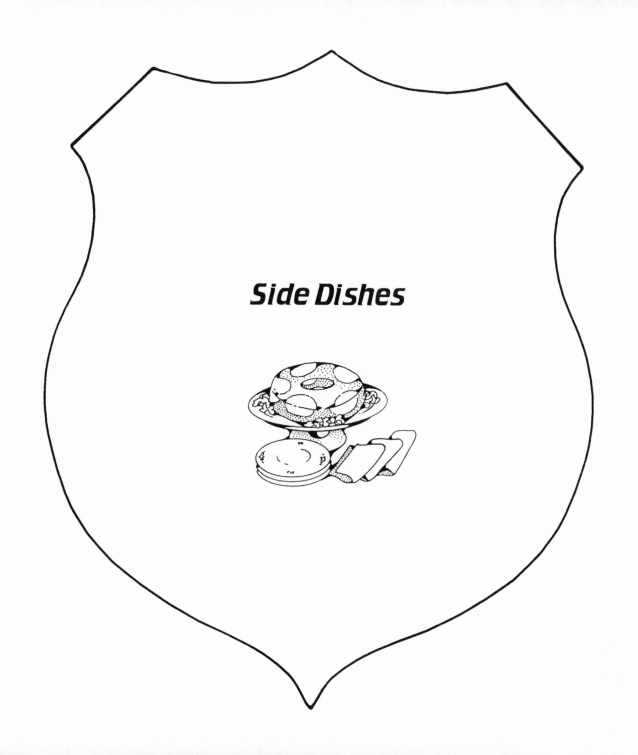

BAKED BEANS

Serves 15-20
Preparation time: 1-1/4 hours

Benton Burt
Chief of Police
Brookhaven, Mississippi

Ingredients:

16 slices bacon, cooked crispy and crumbled
2 large onions, chopped
2 medium bell peppers, chopped
1 gallon Campbells Pork-n-Beans
4 teaspoons garlic powder
8 tablespoons prepared mustard
1-1/2 cups catsup
6 tablespoons Worcestershire sauce
1 cup brown sugar
1 cup maple (or imitation) syrup
Pepper to taste

Utensils:

Frying pan
Large baking dish
Oven, preheat to 350°

① In frying pan, brown bacon. Remove bacon and set aside.

② In frying pan with bacon drippings, saute onions and bell peppers.

③ In baking dish, combine Pork-n-Beans, garlic powder, prepared mustard, catsup, Worcestershire sauce, brown sugar, syrup, onions, bell peppers, and pepper.

④ Bake at 350° for approximately 45 minutes; do not over cook.

Remove from oven and cover with crumbled bacon slices.

BAKED ZUCCHINI & CHEESE

Serves 6-8
Preparation time: 1 hour

Eileen Elhard
Patrol Officer
Bismarck, North Dakota

Ingredients:

3 cups zucchini, coarsely grated
1 large onion, minced
3 slices lean bacon, minced
1 cup cheddar cheese, grated
1 cup self-rising flour
1/2 cup vegetable oil
5 large eggs, beaten lightly
3/4 teaspoon salt
1/2 teaspoon pepper

Utensils:

Mixing bowl
10" x 6" x 2" baking pan
Oven, preheat to 350°

①   In a bowl, combine zucchini, onion, and bacon.

②   Gently stir in cheese, flour, oil, eggs, salt, and pepper until mixed.

③   Pour into buttered baking pan.

④   Bake for 45-50 minutes.

     Substitute self-rising flour with 1 cup flour, 1-1/2 teaspoons baking powder, and 1/2 teaspoon salt.

BROCCOLI SALAD

Serves 8
Preparation time: 6-12 hours

John M. Cropper
Chief of Police
Ridgely, Maryland

Ingredients:

1 bunch broccoli, remove stems
1/2 cup raisins
1 small onion, chopped
12 slices bacon

Dressing:
1 cup mayonnaise
1/4 cup sugar
2 teaspoons vinegar

Utensils:

Frying pan
Large bowl

①   Fry bacon until crisp. Drain off fat and crumble bacon.

②   In a bowl, toss all salad ingredients.

③   Mix mayonnaise, sugar, and vinegar. Pour over salad (do not stir).

④   Refrigerate 6-12 hours.

CALICO BEAN BAKE
Serves 4-6
Preparation time: 1-1/2 hours

Karen A. Bradford
Dispatcher
Smyrna, Tennessee

Ingredients:
1/2 pound ground beef
1/2 pound bacon
1/2 cup onion, chopped
1/2 cup barbeque sauce
2 tablespoons brown sugar
1 teaspoon dry mustard
1 teaspoon vinegar
1, 12 ounce can brown baked beans
1, 16 ounce can red kidney beans
1, 6 ounce can lima beans

Utensils:
Frying pan
Oblong pan or glass dish
Oven, preheat to 375°

①   In frying pan, cook bacon until crisp. Cut into small pieces.

②   Add beef and onion and fry until beef is browned.

③   Combine remaining ingredients and pour into oblong pan.

④   Bake for 1 hour.

CAULIFLOWER IN CURRIED SAUCE

Serves 4-6
Preparation time: 35 minutes

Don Jackson
Sergeant
Buckeye, Arizona

Ingredients:

1, 10-1/2 ounce can cream of mushroom or celery soup
1-1/4 cups longhorn cheese, shredded
1/4 cup mayonnaise
1 teaspoon curry powder
1 large head cauliflower, broken into flowerettes

Utensils:

Saucepan
Mixing bowl
Casserole dish
Oven, preheat to 350°

①   In saucepan, cook cauliflower until tender. Drain.

②   In a bowl, combine soup, cheese, mayonnaise, and curry powder.

③   Put cauliflower in buttered casserole dish. Pour sauce over it.

④   Bake for 30 minutes, until sauce is golden and bubbly.

CHICKEN FRIED RICE
Serves 7-14
Preparation time: 45 minutes

Paul J. Feller
Captain
Dubuque, Iowa

Ingredients:
4 cups cooked rice, prepared ahead of time and refrigerated
1 chicken breast, cut into 1/4" cubes
2 carrots, cut into 1/4" pieces
1 bunch green onions, chopped with some of the greens
1 can waterchestnuts, cut into 1/4" pieces
1 package frozen peas
1 egg, scrambled and cut into strips
1/4 teaspoon garlic powder
1/4 teaspoon ginger powder
2 tablespoons peanut oil

Utensils:
Wok or deep frying pan

Sauce:
2 eggs, slightly beaten
4 tablespoons oyster flavored
  sauce
2 tablespoons soy sauce

① Mix the ingredients for the sauce and set aside.

② In the wok, heat the oil and stir-fry the chicken, adding the garlic and ginger powders. Stir for 2-3 minutes. Remove and drain.

③ Heat more oil and stir-fry carrots and waterchestnuts for 2 minutes. Add onions and stir-fry for 1 more minute.

④ Add chicken and frozen peas and stir-fry for 1 minute; remove and drain.

⑤ Add more oil and stir-fry rice for 2 minutes. Add mixture of chicken and vegetables. While stirring, drizzle in the sauce and mix completely. Mix in scrambled eggs.

This will keep for 7-9 days in the refrigerator.

FILTHY RICE
Serves 10-15
Preparation time: 20 minutes

Martin C. Herring
Patrol Officer
Cambridge, Maryland

Ingredients:

1 pound ground sausage (sage or ham flavored)
1, 16 ounce jar salsa
3 cups rice, cooked
1, 15 ounce can black beans
4 ounces cheddar or Monterey Jack cheese, grated
8 tablespoons sour cream
1 bag tortilla chips or cracker of choice

Utensils:

Frying pan
Shallow serving bowl

①   Brown the sausage and drain.

②   Add the salsa, rice, and black beans and bring to boil.

③   Put in serving bowl and top with cheese and sour cream.

      Serve with chips or crackers and beer.

91

GUACAMOLE DIP

Serves 4-6
Preparation time: 1 hour

Don Jackson
Sergeant
Buckeye, Arizona

Ingredients:

2 medium avocados, peeled, seeded, and diced
1 small tomato, chopped
2 tablespoons onion, minced
1 teaspoon lemon juice
1/2 teaspoon garlic powder
1/2 teaspoon salt

Utensils:

Serving bowl

①   Combine all ingredients.

②   Chill for 45 minutes.

Serve with tortilla chips and beer or as a side dish to a Mexican dinner.

KIELBASA APPETIZER

Serves 8-10
Preparation time: 10 minutes

Mary Ellen O'Connor
Senior Clerk
Beverly, Massachusetts

Ingredients:

2 packages Kielbasa, sliced into bite-size pieces
2 jars Durkee Famous Mustard and Sandwich Sauce
1, 24 ounce bottle maple syrup

Utensils:

Broiler pan
Large saucepan

①   Broil Kielbasa for 5 minutes on each side. Let cool to room temperature.

②   In a saucepan, pour in mustard. Take empty bottles and fill with maple syrup. Pour over mustard.

③   Bring mixture to a boil, mixing well.

④   Add Kielbasa to sauce mixture and refrigerate overnight.

MARINATED CRAB SALAD
Serves 10
Preparation time: 15 minutes

Norman R. "Nookie" Diaz
Chief of Police
Thibodaux, Louisiana

Ingredients:

4 dozen boiled crabs
1 pound onions, ringed
1 large bell pepper, chopped
4 ribs celery, cut in 1" pieces
2 jars Cajun Chef Mild Pepperoncini (mild peppers)
1, 32 ounce jar pickled spiced cauliflowers
2 cups olive oil
6 lemons, squeezed
1 ounce Worcestershire sauce

Utensils:

Large mixing bowl

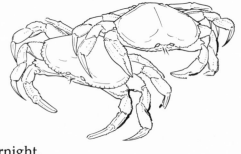

①   Combine the ingredients.

②   Marinate several hours or refrigerate overnight.

MARINATED OYSTERS
Serves 10
Preparation time: 15 minutes

Norman R. "Nookie" Diaz
Chief of Police
Thibodaux, Louisiana

Ingredients:

1 gallon oysters, unwashed
1, 32 ounce jar dill giardiniera
1 jar pickled cauliflower or vegetables
1, 16 ounce bottle catsup
1, 16 ounce bottle Italian salad dressing
2, 5 ounce jars horseradish
1 small bottle Worcestershire sauce
1 large onion, ringed
1 large bell pepper, ringed
1 bunch shallots, chopped
3 ribs celery, cut into 1" pieces
4 cloves garlic, chopped
1 bottle Louisiana Hot sauce
Salt to taste

Utensils:

Extra large bowl or pot

①   Combine the ingredients.

②   Marinate several hours or refrigerate overnight.

RED FRIED RICE

Serves 4-6
Preparation time: 20 minutes

Don Jackson
Sergeant
Buckeye, Arizona

Ingredients:

Minute rice
1/2 pound bacon, sliced
1 medium onion, diced
1/2 cup salsa
1/2 cup catsup
Salt and pepper to taste

Utensils:

Saucepan
Frying pan

①   Prepare rice according to package instructions.

②   Brown bacon and onion.

③   Combine all ingredients.

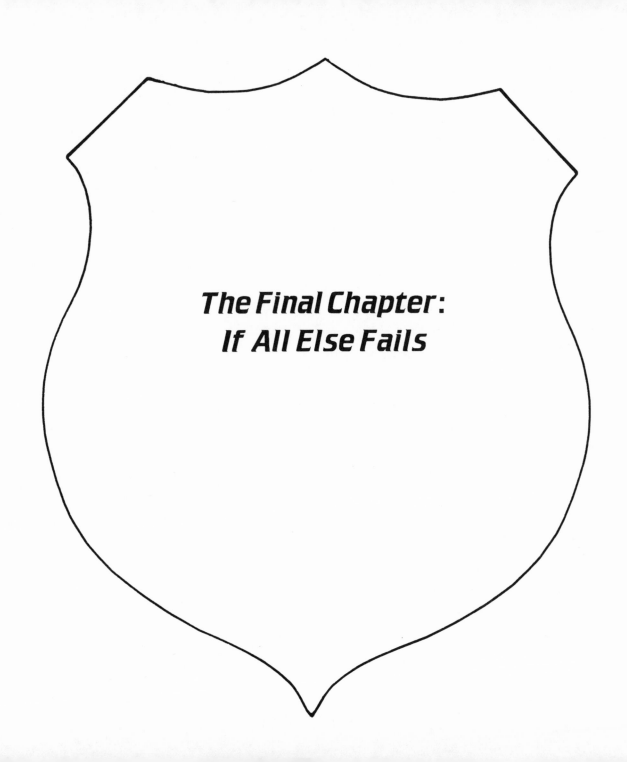

**The Final Chapter:
If All Else Fails**

Sometimes, you just gotta leave the kitchen behind, and I would have been remiss if I left out the most famous of all the 'cop' fast foods:

Donuts from your favorite donut shop!

(*Ah-hem.* I clear my throat; I begin to read.)
"In Pursuit"
a poem by Nadine E. Anderberg

Lookout! A patrol car's screamin'
Lights flashin', sirens blarin'
Wow, maybe a criminal's on the loose
The thrill of a chase, to catch a thief
Draw those guns, handcuff the slime
All in a day's work, not just 9-5
But, look, now I see what the commotion's 'bout
No crime in progress, no emergency
Just a stomach crying in pain
The last meal hours, maybe days ago
Half-eaten, on the run
Rolaids have been the filler
But now a chance to grab a bite:
A pursuit to the local donut shop

(Cheers and clapping. I bow.)

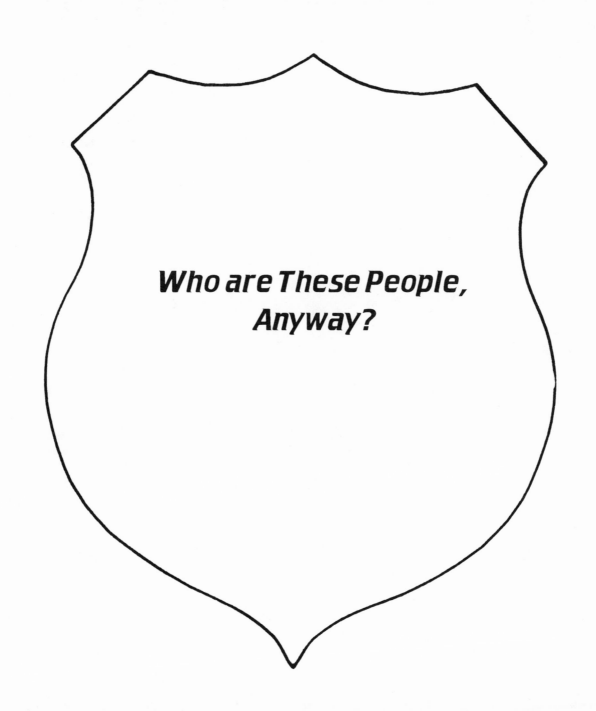

Who are These People, Anyway?

Patrol Officer Bret Anderberg (picture) is assigned to the swing shift at Bloomington Police Department, Minnesota. Bloomington is a city of 81,000, just south of Minneapolis, and home of the "Mall of America". The department has 100 employees. Bret loves to cook and devise new creations. His claim to fame is food that speaks loudly and freely while digesting.

Sergeant Tony Barthuly is assigned to the 3-11 pm shift at Fond du Lac Police Department, Wisconsin. He is also a S.W.A.T Commander, Defensive Tactics Coordinator, and firearms instructor.

Dispatcher Karen A. Bradford (picture) is the TAC and trains dispatchers at the Smyrna Police Department, Tennessee. Her primary interest is cooking nutritious meals and uses the officers as her guinea 'pigs'. After more than 5 years in the department, she hasn't lost one yet and plans to pursue a career in nutrition after she graduates from college. Smyrna Police Department serves a population of 14,700 and has 40 employees.

Secretary Joan P. Carey works with 8 other employees at the Mineral Point Police Department, Wisconsin. Besides her busy work schedule, Joan is putting together a family cookbook; her relatives number in the hundreds!

Chief Deputy Jack L. Dillon (picture) has been in the Washington County Sheriff/Police Department, Iowa, since 1981. The department serves a county over 570 square miles and a population of 20,400. The department has 20 employees. Next to cooking, Jack loves being a grandfather.

Patrol Officer Eileen Elhard (picture) has been a police officer for 15 years. The Bismarck Police Department, North Dakota, has 90 employees and serves a population of 50,000. Eileen loves to cook, eat, and sometimes *wear* the food! She also participates in a gourmet club, where officers share recipes with each other.

Captain Paul J. Feller has been on the Dubuque Police Department, Iowa, over 20 years. His assignments include the third shift commander and patrol officer. The department of 74 employees serves 60,000 people. His only claim to fame is trying to establish a new trend by heating Twinkies in the microwave. It seems that his partner didn't have enough hot food in his diet.

Assistant Chief William F. Gebauer has been second in command in Medford Police Department, Wisconsin, for over 10 years and has over 20 years on the police force. Serving a city of approximately 5,000 people, Medford Police Department employs seven people. William is camera-shy but doesn't mind stealing recipes from his wife, Bonnie.

Detective Brian W. Hart (picture) has been on the West Warwick Police Department, Rhode Island, for 20 years. His only concern is whether anyone would trust a face like his?

Lieutenant Bill Hatton has been on the Victoria Police Department, Texas, for over 20 years. Victoria is located between Houston and Corpus Christi, near the coast, and has a population of 60,000.

Chief Edward Hayes (picture) has been in law enforcement over 20 years. Peekskill Police Department, New York, has 52 employees that serve a city of 20,000 people. Edward enjoys cooking and frequently prepares dishes for parties, while on vacation, and for *anybody* who asks.

Patrol Officer Martin C. Herring (picture) works in the Cambridge Police Department, Maryland, patrol division. He is also a field training officer and a member of the emergency response team. When his wife's away, in the kitchen he plays, creating new recipes that amaze and astound his friends and family. Although they shouldn't be allowed to name his creations!

Sergeant Don Jackson (picture) has been a police officer for 15 years. Buckeye Police Department, Arizona, has a staff of 18 and serves a population of 3,700. Besides loving the activity of cooking, Don has a policy of 'adopting' fellow officers for the purpose of putting on a 'feedbag' every Sunday evening. According to Don, there's nothing better than a "hot home-cooked meal and some good fellowship".

Secretary, Records Section, Denise A. Jenter has worked in several areas of Sturgis Police Department, South Dakota, since 1978. Sturgis has a population of 5,800 and 10 police officers. Denise loves to eat and cook. Since she does both frequently, she has had almost every conceivable mishap, including oven doors blowing open and food exploding! Denise has a speed dial on her phone for 911!

Records Clerk Technician Inez Kashmark has worked at Appleton Police Department, Minnesota, for almost 5 years. The department has four employees and serves the town of 1,800 people.

Chief's Secretary Doris Meredith Larson (picture) has been a Pulaski Police Department employee since 1971. She has worked for five Chiefs of Police. Pulaski has a population of 10,711, and their police department has 23 employees. Doris is known as the "lady with the hats" because she collects them and wears one everyday. But you won't catch her wearing a hat after 6:00 pm unless the weather is cold.

Patrol Officer Charles M. Latham (picture) has been with Fulton Police Department, Missouri, for over a decade. Fulton has a population of 12,000. His favorite 'cop' food is chili. He stated he hasn't been with the department long enough to collect information on the "long term carcinogenic effects" of his chili. Eat at your own risk.

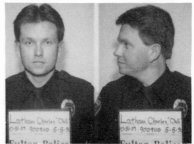

Patrol Officer Lisa Michaelis (picture) has been with Monroe Department, Connecticut, for over a decade. Monroe has a population of 18,000, and the department has 35 employees. Although she *can* be caught working the swing shift, she *won't* be caught eating another meatball grinder on duty or without proper bib attire.

Sergeant Gene P. Plambeck (picture) makes a habit of cooking for officers when he works the midnight shift. Cody Police Department, Wyoming, has a staff of 14 and serves a community of 10,000. The most memorable 'comment' anyone made about his cooking was one of the wives who, after smelling his oyster stew, raced out of the room so she wouldn't throw up!

Chief James B. Simmerman (picture) has 22 employees reporting to him in Marshall Police Department, Missouri. He has been in law enforcement 25 years. His only problem with cooking was telling a guest that he used Kennel Ration to keep his meatloaf together. Unfortunately, the guest didn't keep it together or take it lightly since she had already eaten his dinner. Whata doggoned shame!

Detention Officer Carl Stennes works with a "family" of 30 at Roosevelt County Sheriff's Department, Wolf Point, Montana. Located in the northeast section of the state, Wolf Point is on the Fort Peck Indian Reservation and has a population of 10,000 people.

Patrol Officer Scott A. Stookey has been with the Stillwater Police Department, Oklahoma, for over 10 years. The department has 55 employees. His recipes for two are "served in the nude with light wine or champagne". For larger crowds, he doesn't drink because the dishes are so spicy that the "cook should be armed". When he's not cooking, Scott is writing cop novels; he's on his fourth one!

Chief Ted Vastine (picture) claims that he does not make the French rolls himself, but his mother-in-law and wife do, and "they are responsible for my gaining weight over the past 20 years"...ah, the rolls, that is. Ted did not have time to offer any information about his police department or city, although he was able to dig up a high school photo of himself.

Bureau Secretary Lenora Viveros (picture) works for the Ventura Police Department, California, which has 121 employees. The city's population is 92,750. She is one of the many cooks in the department; several have won blue ribbons at the County Fair for their recipes.

Captain Lawrence A. Wallace (picture) has been with the Kotzebue Police Department, Alaska, since July 1979. Thirty-five miles north of the Arctic Circle, Kotzebue is on the north-west coast of Alaska and is host to 4,000 people. The department has 9 officers. Lawrence's idea of of a good time--besides thinking of unique ways of keeping warm--is to burn hams and explode Pyrex dishes, which in turn burn *his* hands, holes in the the linoleum floor and shag carpet, and ignite fires in the gar-bage. He is also known for stealing recipes from his mother. (He claims the Statute of Limitations is up.) Do you feel safe with this guy around?

Records Clerk Stephanie D. Yutzie has also worked as a dispatcher for Walla Walla Police Department, Washington. Working shifts prevents her from spending a lot of time cooking nutritious meals for herself and husband, Officer Charles. But, by using quick cooking methods, she now 'nukes' nutritious meals in a microwave.

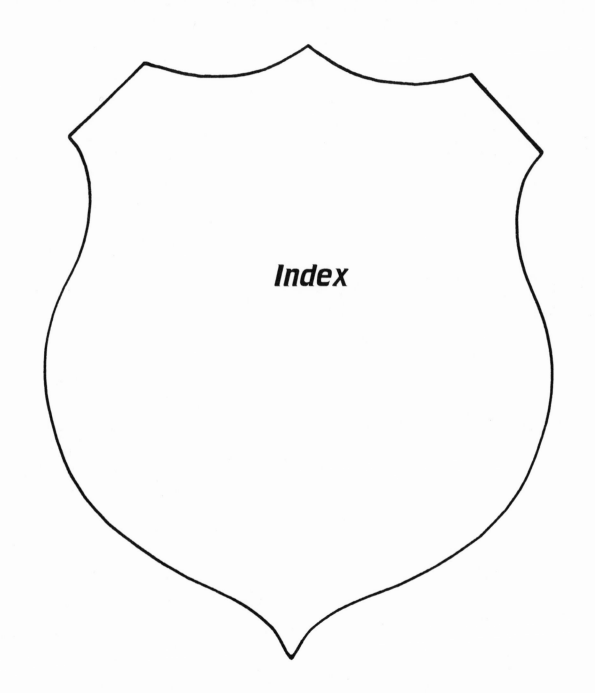

Index

WANT MORE GREAT COOKING??? SURE!

"True Southern Family Recipes: The Joy of Home Cooking" by Drew Weeks. Most of these one-of-a-kind, family-tested meals can be prepared quickly, and then saved for later. Price $14.95. Order Number 922-9.

"The Lowfat Mexican Cookbook: True Mexican Taste Without the WAIST" by Robert Leos and Nancy Leos. If you love Mexican foods as much as we do, but do not want the extra calories it contains, then this is just what the chef needs. Good eating as well as good health are here in this great little book. Price $6.95. Order Number 896.

"This For That: A Treasury of Savvy Substitutions for the Creative Cook" by Meryl Nelson. Meryl's cookbooks are nationally famous. *This For That* has been featured in Family Circle and many other national publications, TV and radio. Hints, Recipes, How-To's for using THIS when you're out of THAT, includes microwave directions. Price $6.95. Order Number 847.

"The Newlywed Cookbook" by Robin Walsh. Bet you have a wedding to go to soon—here is the perfect wedding gift to add to a set of hand towels or an appliance. *The Newlywed Cookbook* is the perfect kitchen gift along with our other titles listed here. The Famous *Chef Tell* says, "Amusing, creative ideas for the beginner cook. I highly recommend it!" Price $12.95. Order Number 877.

"Your One Year Diet Diary: An Easy-To-Keep Daily Record of Your Successes" by Diane J. Mentzer. If you're fed up with diets that don't work, then this special little book can help you to take control of your eating, and lose weight permanently. Price $6.95. Order Number 928-8.